Listening *for* God

Silence Practice for
Little Ones

By Katie Warner
Illustrated by Amy Rodriguez

For Ma and Dad Warner & the Schoellhammers.
Blessed to be able to call you family.
- K.W.

With love, to my brother, Chris
- A.R.

And he said, "Go forth, and stand upon the mount before the LORD." And behold, the LORD passed by, and a great and strong wind rent the mountains, and broke in pieces the rocks before the LORD, but the LORD was not in the wind; and after the wind an earthquake, but the LORD was not in the earthquake; and after the earthquake a fire, but the LORD was not in the fire; and after the fire a still small voice.

1 Kings 19:11-12

Book design by Meg Whalen. The text for this book is set in Questa. The illustrations for this book were rendered in Photoshop.

ISBN: 978-1-5051-1892-6

Published in the United States by
TAN Books · PO Box 269 · Gastonia, NC · 28053
www.TANBooks.com
Printed and bound in India

A long time ago,
there lived a man named Elijah
who loved God with all his heart.

Elijah was one of
God's prophets. Through Elijah, God
gave messages of love, repentance,
and mercy to his chosen people.

One night,
weary and despairing
from the hard work of
sharing God's messages
only to be rejected by
others, Elijah lay down
to rest under the
shade of a broom
tree.

He waited to hear God's voice,
needing hope and strength to live the life
that God was calling him to live.

An angel of the Lord appeared to Elijah,
beckoning him to eat, drink, and keep going on his journey.

Elijah slowly made his way to Mount Horeb,
the same mountain—also called Sinai—
where God made his presence known to
Moses and the Israelites.

There Elijah stood.

But where was God?

Suddenly, a strong wind came upon the mountain,
breaking the rocks into pieces all around Elijah.

But God was not in the wind.

Next, an earthquake shook the mountain,
where Elijah stood in its tremble.

But God was not in the earthquake.

Then came fire, roaring
and encircling the waiting Elijah.

But God was not in the fire.

After the fire, all was quiet.

And then,
in the silence,
Elijah heard a still small voice.

It was God.

This story of finding God in the silence is not just Elijah's story.
It's your story too.

God wants to make his presence known to you.
He wants to speak to you!

God wants to give you faith, hope, love, wisdom, courage, and
strength to live the life he is calling you to live.

He has a special plan for you,
just like he had a special plan for Elijah.

Your job is to listen for him.

You have to learn to be quiet and still
so you can hear God's still small voice.

Let's try this together...

Can you stand up and be the wind?
Swirl your arms around
and blow air from your mouth,
strong like the mighty wind.

Can you be an earthquake?
Stomp your feet and
rumble the ground
like a big, shaky
earthquake.

Can you be fire?
Crouch down...

... then jump up
with your hands above
your head and **ROAR**,
like a flame growing into a
raging fire.

Now be still.

Sit down and relax your body.
Quiet your voice and your mind.
Take a deep breath in and let it out.

Now listen to the silence.

We are going to sit here in silence for a few minutes.
Keep your body still,
your heart open,
and your voice quiet.
Just listen to the silence.
I'll let you know when we are finished.

Our sacred silent time starts now.

That was great.
Sometimes being silent can be hard,
but it is so important to practice it.
When we practice being silent,
we ready ourselves to hear God speaking to us in
our lives.

In the silence, we wait for him to show us
his adventurous plan for us.

There is a wonderful end to Elijah's story:
he became a great saint with God in heaven.
God has that desire for you too—
to be a saint with him in heaven someday!

Keep practicing that sacred silence
and listening for God's still small voice every day.

He will lead you and guide you,
and like Elijah,
you too can do great things for God.

A note to the adults

Years ago, I started having my young children practice silent time each day.

They loved the story of Elijah and the still small voice. I'd ask them, "Did Elijah hear God in the wind?" "NO!!!" they'd yell excitedly.

"How about in the earthquake?" "NO!"

"In the fire?" "NO!"

"How did Elijah hear God?" I wondered. Their voices hushed and their eagerness grew as they'd whisper, "In the still small voice."

That daily practice became the seed concept for this book. I think it's so important for little ones to learn early and intentionally how to quiet themselves so they can hear God's voice. At first, our silent time training only lasted a minute. Then two, three, four...

They look forward to it now as a regular staple of our prayer time. Now, don't picture a perfectly silent atmosphere in our home as you'd find in a monastery—if the young toddler is anywhere nearby, there is definitely background noise, and the three-yea- old usually whispers, "Has it been five minutes yet?" at least twice. But it's such a helpful start, a building block to future holy hours that our little ones will spend in the adoration chapel or at home listening for God's voice and getting to know their Savior and Best Friend.

Cardinal Robert Sarah writes, "God achieves everything, acts in all circumstances, and brings about all our interior transformations. But he does it when we wait for him in recollection and silence."

The ability to be silent is a skill that many adults don't even cultivate. Let's give this priceless gift of cultivating silence to our children early. I believe it is a gift that will reap rewards beyond our wildest imaginations.

Praying for you and your little disciples,

Katie Warner

P.S. If your children ever get discouraged during silent time because they don't hear God's audible voice, remind them of God's love for them! He wants to speak to their hearts and the more we practice listening for him, the more we prepare our hearts to hear his voice. But also remind them of the other ways God speaks to us, like through his Word (the Bible), through other people, and through the blessings he gives us (like a beautiful rainbow). We can be listening for God's voice in our lives all the time! He IS talking to us!